DESTINATION
DELHI

Published in 2011 by
Prakash Books India Pvt. Ltd.
1, Ansari Road, Daryaganj, New Delhi-110 002, India
Tel.: 2324 7062-65, Fax: 2324 6975
E-mail: sales@prakashbooks.com
Website: www.prakashbooks.com

ISBN : 978 81 7234 362 0

Printed & bound in India at: Rave india
www.raveindiapress.com

DESTINATION
DELHI

SUJIT SANYAL

PRAKASH BOOKS

DELHI
A DESTINATION IN HISTORY

Located at the epicenter of the Indian subcontinent's history for the past 800 years, Delhi is an ever-expanding metropolis which is a seamless blend of the traditional and the contemporary. Unlike other great cities of the past, it is still emerging in its character, passing through a series of metamorphoses.

What was the capital of a chieftain in the 15th century, became the focal point of all Muslim invaders, with major wars and battles being fought with regular periodicity. Delhi saw a change of seven major dynasties, culminating as the capital of the British India in 1911.

LODI GARDENS. DELHI IS FULL OF SUCH HISTORICAL MONUMENTS THAT ADD TO THE
ARCHITECTURE OF THE CITY. OPPOSITE PAGE: THE GATES OF POWER. RASHTRAPATI BHAWAN
THROUGH THE MAIN GATE ON RAISINA HILL.

For the past 60 years, Delhi has symbolized the development, both economic and social, of a great nation. A nation that has been able to withstand the test of time, specially the trials of a very difficult financial crisis that the world had been going through.

The city is full of monuments and beautiful gardens, is rich in architecture, is also the seat of political power, and after Mumbai, is the major industrial and commercial centre of India. It is, therefore, unique, and boasts of a culture that is a convergence of different footprints made by an array of rulers, the last being the British.

The city has witnessed the plunders by Tamerlane and later, Nadir Shah; the establishment of the Mughal dynasty by Babur; the crushing of the Indian Mutiny by the British; the assassination of Mahatma Gandhi[1] and Indira Gandhi[2]. It has hosted two Asian Games (1951 & 1982) and now there are the Commonwealth Games in 2010. It is the fashion capital of India with major designers having their boutiques here, and the entire region being dotted with shopping malls and multiplexes. Food is an integral part of the city and while all kinds of cuisines are available, the city has its own

---

[1] At the Birla House, Tees January Marg, on January 30, 1948

[2] At 1, Safdarjung Road, the then Prime Minister's residence on October 30, 1984

MAN PAYS HIS RESPECTS AT THE GANDHI MEMORIAL AT RAJGHAT.

brand of dishes – a mix and match of robust North-Western, Mughlai and Punjabi cuisine. It is a city of food lovers, which speaks for itself through the city's multitudinous eateries; some of which like 'Karim's', have attained a legendary status. Being in the country's capital, you have access to all types of food: Italian, Tex-Mex, Greek, French, and of course, all kinds of Indian cuisines. The pub culture is a part of the neo-lifestyle, and with the Government relaxing rules, the city boasts of some of the best pubs in India.

MODERN-DAY MALL AT AN UPMARKET DELHI ADDRESS. THE MALLS HAVE CHANGED THE
LIFESTYLE AND SHOPPING HABITS OF THE RESIDENTS OF DELHI-NCR.

The inhabitants of Delhi truly represent the people of India. To the original inhabitants namely, the Jats, Gujjars, Rajputs, were added the invading communities of the Mongols, now known as Mughals, Afghans, while the Sikhs, being in close proximity to their homeland Punjab, represent a sizeable section of the population. The Hindu community is made up of those commonly called 'Punjabis', many of whom are early settlers while many more joined in after the partition of the country in 1947. From 1911, the city has seen an influx of people from different parts of the country. First, the Bengalis,

many of whom came with Government jobs when the capital shifted to Delhi (earlier, the capital was Kolkata), and with jobs in administration, judiciary and the like, followed the others. Post-independence, the populace from other parts of the country flowed in large numbers, and settled in different pockets of the city. Chittaranjan Park is the mini-Bengal, Pushp Vihar is the Delhi's Malayalee[1] address.

---

[1] Malayalee: A very industrious and very educated set of people from the coastal state of Kerala in South India. Kerala, famous for tourist spots, is the only state in India to have attained 100% literacy level.

COLOURFUL VIGNETTES OF THE CITY. DELHI IS FULL OF LIVELY, HARD-WORKING PEOPLE, EVER FORTHCOMING WITH HELP OR JUST A FRIENDLY CHAT.

Delhi is home to some of the major business houses in India. The Nandas, the Shrirams, the Thapars; also, Ranbaxy have had their corporate offices in Delhi, and today Delhi is the Country Office in India to many MNCs (multi-national companies).

While this book restricts itself to Delhi per se, Delhi is a part of the National Capital Region (NCR) which consists of Delhi, Gurgaon, Faridabad and Noida, as they are adjacent to the city borders, and though located outside the political boundary of the state of Delhi, have a seamless infrastructure to facilitate growth and services.

People living in different cities in the NCR work in other cities, and there are porous borders to create ease of movement.

The city of Delhi has been a major seat of learning in modern India. Other than Delhi University, which covers 83 colleges and the famous Delhi School of Economics, which had Dr. Manmohan Singh, India's Prime Minister and Nobel Laureate Prof, Amartya Sen in the teaching faculty, Delhi also houses Jamia Milia Islamia University, Jawaharlal Nehru University and Indira Gandhi National Open University. The National School of Drama (NSD) has produced some of India's leading film stars while the School of Architecture is one of the famed prestigious institutions in India. Over the past two decades, a large number of Management Schools have been set up in Delhi-NCR region, some of which are ranked amongst the top ten in the country.

DELHI-NCR IS VERY WELL-CONNECTED WITH METRO TRANSPORT NETWORK, JOINING ALL ENDS OF THE CITY AND GOING INTO NEIGHBOURING REGIONS OF HARYANA AND UTTAR PRADESH. OPPOSITE PAGE: A RAILWAY PLATFORM AT A DELHI STATION. THE CITY RECEIVES THOUSANDS OF VISITORS EVERY DAY, SOME TOURISTS AND SOME WHO COME FROM ALL OVER THE COUNTRY TO SEEK FAME AND AT TIMES, FORTUNE!

If the pub culture has been a recent phenomenon in the life of Delhi, so has been the growth of medical services. Throughout the NCR, a fresh new industry of world-class medical services has sprung up, the various state governments have allotted special land category for the development of medical hubs, and the services offered by them are comparable to the best in the world.

If politics, infrastructure, business, education are the wheels on which Delhi has been moving, it's not surprising that to many, Delhi has been the centre of cultural and intellectual activities. The

GRAND VIEW OF THE SEAT OF POWER. THE NORTH BLOCK AND THE SOUTH BLOCK,
WHICH HOUSE THE KEY MINISTRIES IN THE ADMINISTRATION.

foresight of the country's first Education Minister[1] has paid rich dividends. The National Gallery of Modern Art (NGMA) is India's premier art storehouse which stocks works of Modern Art from 1850s onward, and has developed galleries for permanent display. The gallery is a repository of the cultural ethos of the country and showcases the changing art forms through the passage of the last hundred and fifty years starting from about 1857 in the field of Visual and Plastic arts. The NGMA collection has some of the finest works of the Bengal School of Painting as well as those of Amrita Sher Gill, Souza, Hussain & Subrahmanyan, to name a few.

---

[1] Maulana Abul Kalam Azad

FOLLOWING PAGES: DELHI-6 – PANORAMIC VIEW OF THE OLD CITY FROM THE JAMA MASJID.

A couple of kilometres away from the NGMA, is the Mandi House complex. Other than being the main office and studio of country's official TV channel, Doordarshan, it is also the centre of theatre and stage shows. A large number of theatres are located around the roundabout as here is also the National School of Drama, with theatre festivals being organized periodically. The English

Theatre, though somewhat elitist, also has its presence in the city.

A unique mixture of various facets of life, Delhi continues to grow with its traditional values and age-old heritage while side-by-side, the metropolis is thriving to become one of the finest, modern and planned cities in the world.

1

THE FORTIFIED ENTRANCE OF THE PURANA QILA, OR OLD FORT. SOME BELIEVE, THIS MAY HAVE BEEN THE SITE OF INDRAPRASTHA, THE PALACE OF THE PANDAVAS IN THE EPIC MAHABHARATA.

In the last thousand years, Delhi has been ruled by a varied lot of emperors, who barring the first one, where all invaders from foreign lands. Some were benevolent, some plunderers; some were builders, poets, while some kept shifting their capital city within the city. One of them shifted to a city in South India, only to return after two years! In fact, Delhi is labelled as a 'City of Seven Capitals', though historians, applying clauses and sub-clauses, have taken the figure up to ten!

The central figure of the Chauhans, who ruled Delhi at the beginning of the 12th century, was Prithviraj Chauhan (1166 – 1192), also known as Rai Pithora. He is the second last Hindu king to rule India (the last being King Hemu who was defeated by Akbar the Great at the Second Battle of Panipat, 1556) before India went under the sword of a series of invaders and thanks to his love for his cousin Sanyukta, is a matter of folklore.

Prithviraj Chauhan ruled jointly from Ajmer and Delhi, and politically, had tried to unify the Rajput rulers against the Mughals. He went on to defeat Afghan invader Mohammad Ghori, in the first battle of Tarrain (in fact, Prithviraj was chivalrous enough to let Ghori go away after defeating him) but was subsequently defeated the very next year, and Delhi came under Muslim rule.

Prithviraj Chauhan expanded Lal Kot built by the Tomars and made it his capital. It was called Qila Rai Pithora. He built huge ramparts and had 13 gates around it, of which only three remain.

Mohammad Ghori, after defeating Prithviraj had no desire to return to India. Instead he sent his slave general, Qutub-ud-din Aibak as his viceroy, and Delhi came under the spell of Muslim domination which lasted till 1857.

Sold as a slave to Mohammad Ghori, Qutub-ud-din was instrumental in the sacking of Delhi in 1193 AD, and subsequently when Ghori was busy consolidating his empire in Central Asia, he was left with the affairs of governing Northern India.

After the establishment of the Delhi Sultanate, one of the first tasks undertaken by Qutub-ud-din Aibak was to destroy all Hindu structures, and as a result, all temples in Lal Kot and Qila Rai Pithora were razed to the ground. A site of an old Vishnu temple became the site for the first mosque in Delhi. After converting some of the temples into mosques, he set about building the Qutub Minar. He died in 1206, interestingly, while playing a game of polo!

The Slave dynasty, which collapsed subsequently, had an interesting ruler in one of the successors. A lady queen in Razia Sultana, who was brave and liberal, and even tolerant of Hindus. Though she was an able administrator, the problem around her was created by the rumoured affair she supposedly had with a

THE WALLS OF TIME –
ARCHED PASSAGEWAYS AT
THE PURANA QILA.

non-Turkish, Habshi slave, who was the keeper of the stable. A state intrigue saw her being overthrown and killed in 1240.

Following the end of the Slave dynasty, Delhi came under the spell of Jalal-ud-din Feroze, the first Khilji ruler.

The Khiljis were a member of the Turkish clan, which was founded by Shaista Khan. Jalal-ud-din was at one time the prime minister and commander to the last Slave monarch, Kaikubad, but killed his master and his baby son to assume power. Born Malik Firuz, Jalal-ud-din, who reigned between 1290 and 1296 and made Kilokri his capital, and defeated a horde of 100,000 Mongols who invaded India.

The most successful Khilji ruler was, of course, Ala-ud-din Khilji, who extended his empire into Deccan and even Tamil Nadu. Ala-ud-din founded Siri, the second, or perhaps, the third city of Delhi.

The Khilji reign ended in 1321, when Ghiyas-ud-din Tughlaq, an ex-slave of Turkish and Mongol origin, assumed power.

The Tughlaqs ruled from 1321 to 1414, but during this period, almost hundred years, there were three Tughlaq rulers who really left their mark: Ghiyas-ud-din, Mohammad Bin Tughlaq and Firoz Shah Tughlaq. Ghiyas-ud-din moved his capital to Tughlaqabad where he created a fortress. Across the fortress, he built his own tomb, in the centre of an artificial lake. The story goes that saint Hazrat Nizamuddin, who had in many ways opposed Ghiyas-ud-din, had predicted that Tughlaqabad would ultimately turn into ruins and become the abode of Gujjars (cowherds, who were then known as robbers) and jackals. In 1325, Ghiyas-ud-din while returning from a military campaign in Bengal died when a pillar of a pavilion constructed to greet him was knocked down by an elephant and landed on the monarch. He rests in the tomb he had built for himself. In

THE QUTUB MINAR, AN ICONIC MONUMENT OF DELHI.

1327 AD, his successor, Mohammad Bin Tughlaq shifted out of Tughlaqabad, citing poor quality of water in that region.

It remains an awesome, grand structure, cutting across almost 7 kms perimeter.

Mohammad Bin Tughlaq was succeeded by his cousin Firoz Shah Tughlaq, who was born of a Hindu mother. He was already in his forties when he took over in 1351, and dug canals and built hospitals, *madrasas* (Muslim schools), parks and removed the tax levied on Hindu Brahmins and did not indulge in any expansion of the empire. He was liberal in many ways, as he had Hindu religious works translated into Persian. He even repaired and built two more storeys of the Qutub Minar, and brought two Ashokan Pillars from Punjab to Delhi, one of which still stands at Feroz Shah Kotla. He died in 1388 at the age of ninety.

THE FINELY CHISELLED WALLS AT THE QUTUB MINAR HAVE STOOD THE TEST OF TIME.

OPPOSITE PAGE:
INTRICATELY CARVED STONE PILLARS, IMMORTAL WORK BY CRAFTSMEN AT THE QUTUB MINAR.

RUINS OF THE ONCE MAJESTIC TUGHLAQABAD.

Nine years after the death of Firoz Shah, Taimur Lang, (shot in the foot by an arrow, he was lame) during the reign of Nasiruddin Mohammad Tughlaq, entered Delhi and massacred the city for fifteen days.

After the sacking of Delhi by Taimur Lang, his emissary, Khizr Khan, who was earlier the governor of Lahore and Multan, acquired Delhi but by then, there were too many rulers, independent of each other, who ruled various parts of Central and West India, and Delhi Sultanate was just one of them. Khizr Khan, titled as 'Shah of Delhi', ruled in the name of Taimur Lang for seven years (1414-1421) and laid the foundation of the Sayyid dynasty. They claimed that they were a descendent of the Prophet of Islam, and hence the name 'Sayyid'. He was a good man. However, his son Mubarak Shah, who succeeded him, spent most of his time handling rebellions (1421-1434) and left his mark in the city by creating a township, Kotla Mubarakpur. He is also said to have founded a city on the banks of Yamuna called Mubarakabad, but there are no traces of this city.

He was murdered and the subsequent successors, in fact two of them, had a very brief tenure. The Delhi Sultanate had shrunk to the area between Palam (where the current international airport is located) and Delhi, and the Sayyids' reign ended in 1451 when the last Sayyid monarch, Alam Shah abdicated in favour of an Afghan chieftain, Malik Bahlol Lodi.

Bahlol Lodi did try to regain the lost glory of Delhi, whose territory was now limited between Punjab to Varanasi. However, his son and successor Sikandar Lodi moved the capital to Sikandra, just on the periphery of Agra (the great Mughal emperor Akbar's tomb is located at Sikandra).

A palace intrigue saw Sikandar's successor Ibrahim Lodi's cousin invite the Mongol chief Babur to India; and in 1526, in

what is known as the 'First Battle of Panipat', about 80 kms from Delhi, Babur defeated Ibrahim Lodi and went on to lay the foundation of the Mughal dynasty which ruled India for 300 years. Ibrahim Lodi's body was buried in the battlefield itself, the only Muslim ruler of Delhi to be killed in a battlefield. The rule was uninterrupted except for a brief 15 years when the Afghan invader, Sher Shah Suri, defeated Humayun, and with his son Islam Sher, ruled Delhi.

Babur's lineage was impeccable. On his mother's side, he was the direct descendant of the Mongol warlord Chenghis Khan (also known as Ghenghis Khan), and on his father's side, Taimur Lang.

Babur was a brilliant strategist of war. He laid a trap for Ibrahim Lodi and lured him into an attack, but Ibrahim Lodi thought otherwise. Lodi's thinking was that it was the duty of the attacker to make the first move and his job was to prevent him from entering Delhi. However, Babur finally had his way, and though he was scornful of Lodi before the battle, he saluted him when his men brought the severed head of Ibrahim Lodi as a trophy. It was ironic that the same person was an author, a music composer, a horticulturist, and had created a new style of calligraphy called Baburi.

Babur died in 1530 and was laid to rest in Agra, opposite to where the Taj would come up one day. Later, his remains were transferred to Kabul as per his last wishes.

Babur's son, Humayun, was a skilled mathematician and keenly into astronomy and astrology. His major military involvement was fighting Sher Shah, an Afghan chief, who defeated him near Agra. For fifteen years, he led a perilous life, wandering all over Sind and Rajasthan, living a life of abject penury.

However, he returned to India in 1554 virtually without any opposition. Back in Delhi, he refurbished the Sher Mahal, one of Sher Shah's palaces (now known as Purana Qila), where he also set up a huge library and an observatory.

The fighting over and the Emperor now in control, Humayun wanted to bring about a series of reforms in the administrative system. One evening, after discussing the planetary positions on the roof of Sher Mahal, he was returning to his quarters when he heard the muezzin call for prayers. He was going down the staircase which was narrow, and as he was preparing to sit on the steps till "the crier had done", he tripped and fell on his head. Three days later, he died. His body rests at Humayun Tomb, a magnificent mausoleum on the banks of Yamuna, now a World Heritage Site.

Humayun was succeeded by his son, Akbar, who probably has been the most illustrious of the Mughal rulers. He not only made truce with the Rajput kings, but also formulated a secular religion called Din-e-Ilahi and consolidated the Mughal Empire to cover all of North and Central India. His personal talents were many, one of which was animal training. He was also a good carpenter and a lace maker. He was also very fond of wrestling. He was fond of fruits, and towards the end of his life had turned into a vegetarian, and encouraged inter-religious discourses. He had a fabled counsel of nine ministers, something like King Arthur, known as *Navaratna*. This included Abul Fazl, who chronicled Akbar's rule; Mian Tansen, the musician; Birbal, the legendary wit; and Raja Todar Mal, who looked after his finances.

Akbar had started work on his tomb at Sikandra, where he was buried after his death in 1605. However, eighty-six years later while his great grandson Aurangzeb was busy stretching the frontiers to Deccan, a band of Jats, inhabitants of the area, entered the mausoleum, plundered it, dragged out the bones of Akbar and threw them into fire.

Akbar was succeeded by his son Jehangir, Akbar's third and eldest surviving son. He had once openly revolted against Akbar in 1600, and though Akbar had decided against Jehangir as his successor, he had at the time of his death signalled to let Jehangir succeed him. He was a patron of the arts, and thus the Mughal miniature paintings flourished. He had also set up a "golden chain of justice" whereby if anyone could pull a chain of sixty bells outside the Agra Fort, they could get a hearing from the Emperor himself. However, he was fond of liquor, and it is said that his wife, Nur Jehan, was the real ruler behind the throne. He died in 1627 and lies buried in Shahdara Bagh at Lahore.

Shah Jahan, who succeeded Jehangir, was really the Great Mughal. He was a prolific builder and built the Taj Mahal, and was the first Mughal monarch who had made Delhi his base. His major contribution was two of Delhi's greatest landmarks: The Red Fort and the Jama Masjid. He made a new capital for himself calling it Shahjahanabad, and the Red Fort was his

ABOVE:
PLAY OF SHADOWS AND LIGHT THROUGH A LATTICE-WORKED WINDOW AT THE HUMAYUN'S TOMB.

BELOW:
A VIEW OF THE DOME FROM THE INSIDE.

palace. No other Mughal king had so much to contribute to the architecture of Delhi as Shah Jahan. Other than Delhi, Shah Jahan also built the Shalimar Gardens at Lahore and the famed Peacock Throne also happened in his reign. His rule came to an abrupt end as internal strife started breaking up the kingdom, and he was put under house arrest by his son Aurangzeb. He died in 1666 and is buried in The Taj Mahal next to his wife.

Aurangzeb, who virtually took power in his hands, was the longest serving Mughal emperor, and continued with Delhi as the capital. He was an able administrator and had several positions as Governor of various provinces under his father. He was unimaginative, had no vision but had ambition. An otherwise simple man, he ruled by the Islamic laws. His only

ISLAMIC-STYLE ARCHES AT
THE RED FORT.

PREVIOUS PAGES:
PRAYER TIME AT
THE JAMA MASJID.

notable contribution to the city of Delhi was the Moti Masjid inside the Red Fort complex. He died in Ahmednagar at the age of 88 in 1707.

Following the death of Aurangzeb, the Mughal Empire started losing its gleam. The exchequer was hit due to the cost of expansions and building monuments. Post-Aurangzeb, there were no strong rulers and India's history slowly changed its face with the advent of The East India Company. Though Delhi remained the capital of the Mughals, they were merely figureheads, and port cities like Kolkata, Chennai and Mumbai started becoming the major trading and administrative points in India. In between, Nadir Shah (1739) and Ahmad Shah Abdali (1761) invaded and plundered Delhi. Nadir Shah is reputed to have taken away the Peacock Throne and the famed 'Koh-i-Noor' Diamond from India. There was no strong leadership and even the Marathas sacked Delhi. In 1804, the Emperor, Shah Alam II requested for protection from the British East India Company, and he virtually became the Emperor of Delhi, extending between Palam and Shahjahanabad. The Mughal Army was also disbanded.

Sadly, the last major Mughal emperor, Bahadur Shah Zafar, could have made a big difference in the history of India. In 1857, during the Sepoy Mutiny, also known as 'The First War of Independence', the mutineers veered around him as

ABOVE:
THE MOTI MASJID, OR PEARL MOSQUE, AT THE RED FORT.

BELOW:
THE MAJESTIC RED FORT, BUILT ENTIRELY OF RED SANDSTONE.

the symbol of a unified India, and requested him to provide leadership against the British, but the poet king, who was not into statecraft dithered, declined, and escaped from the Red Fort, and took refuge in the basement of Humayun's Tomb (in the servants' quarters). And when he was planning to flee Delhi on his own by the river, he was betrayed by his very men and arrested. The British thought it was best to do away with the institution once and for all, and deported him to Burma. The last Mughal ruler died in Yangon where he lies buried.

Following 1857, there is not much Delhi's history as under the Raj. Kolkata became the capital of India till 1911; the British shifted the capital to Delhi and 'New Delhi' was born. The Viceroy started operating from Delhi, so did the administration.

The foundation of the new city was laid in 1911 during the Delhi Durbar by George V (popularly known as 'Pancham Thaat') and Queen Mary, and the job entrusted to two of the Empire's best architects, Edwin Lutyens and Herbert Baker. Though both Lutyens and Baker worked on the new buildings which included the Viceroy's House (now Rashtrapati Bhawan), the Secretariat buildings, the Parliament House. "New" Delhi came to be known as 'Lutyens' Delhi'.

With the capital having moved to New Delhi, it became the centre of all political activities for India's struggle for freedom. It was here, where the final talks failed between Gandhi, Jinnah and other Congress Party leaders, leading to the establishment of Pakistan. The final touches to the blueprint of independence were drawn up here, and on the midnight of August 14th, India kept its tryst with destiny.

Sadly, a few months later, on January 30, 1948, Mahatma Gandhi, the apostle of peace was assassinated at the Birla House in New Delhi. On October 30, 1984, India witnessed another assassination in New Delhi, that of the Prime Minister, Indira Gandhi.

In the changing dynamics of international politics, New Delhi, now the capital of one of the fast emerging economic powers, continues to create history. Every day...

ABOVE:
PARLIAMENT BUILDING:
THE SEAT OF THE WORLD'S
LARGEST DEMOCRACY.

BELOW:
INDIA ON SHOW AT THE
REPUBLIC DAY PARADE
ON RAJPATH.

PEOPLE 40–51

THE WOMAN WITH THE RED TRUNK PERCHED ON HER HEAD IS, IN ALL PROBABILITY, GOING TO DROP HER
SON TO SCHOOL, AND THEN GET TO WORK SETTING SHOP ON A PAVEMENT, THE WARES OF WHICH THE TRUNK
HOLDS. PAGE 40: LIVING THE PRESENT WITH THE PAST. A BUSY ROAD OUTSIDE THE RED FORT. RICKSHAWS ARE A
POPULAR MODE OF TRANSPORT FOR THE COMMON MAN.

Delhi is a melting pot of different cultures and communities of people from all over the country and even foreign lands. The city began with Jats, Gujjars and Rajputs as its inhabitants. With the Afghan and Mughal invasions, Muslims were added to the city's colourful culture. Sikhs form a large part of the boisterous and jolly population of Punjabis famous for their expansive celebration of life and their magnanimous view of things. With the coming in of the British, Delhi saw a certain amount of conversions to the Christian faith. When the British moved the capital from Kolkata to Delhi in 1911, the city saw an influx of Bengalis who held positions in the government or the judiciary and hence, moved to Delhi. Over the years, people from all over the country have flocked to the capital for better jobs and opportunities and for a better standard of life.

Many Marwaris who originally came from Rajasthan, and also the Baniyas of Uttar Pradesh and Bihar, have made Delhi their home. They are a highly enterprising class of people and certainly very successful businessmen and merchants. Predominantly Hindus and Jains, they are strict vegetarians and staunchly religious, frequently donating large sums of money to temples and organizing religious functions. Many a business house in Delhi, you will find, is run by an Agarwal, Oswal, Goyal, Mittal or Jain. Some very successful businessmen of Delhi are Sunil Mittal of Bharti Airtel, Savitri Jindal of Jindal Steel, and Pradeep Jain of Parsvnath Developers.

A number of skilled engineers, scientists and software professionals, from the south have set base in Delhi, working with the many multinational corporations that have their India offices in the capital.

THE COMMON MAN – DREAMING, PRAYING, GROOMING, LOADING, BUT STILL SMILING.

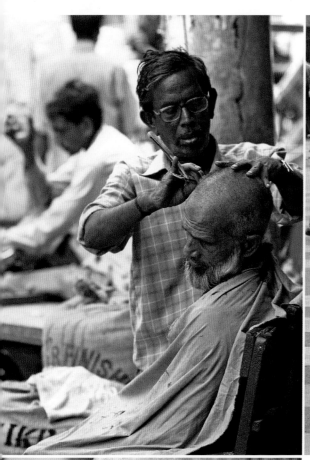

BLESSED WATERS QUENCH ONE'S THIRST AND ASSURE A SENSE OF PEACE.

OPPOSITE PAGE,
ABOVE:
OCTOBER ONWARDS BEGINS THE FESTIVE SEASON, AND FESTIVE DRY FRUITS AND NUTS ARE A MUST IN EVERY HOUSEHOLD.
BELOW, LEFT:
OF POPCORNS, PEANUTS AND JOLLY GOSSIP. THE HEART-WARMING LOHRI BONFIRE.
BELOW, RIGHT:
CRACKERS GALORE AT A BRIGHT DIWALI.

And therefore, as mostly every community in India has its own selective pockets in Delhi, every festival is celebrated with equal enthusiasm and celebration – be it Onam for the Malayalees, Durga Puja for the Bengalis, Eid for the Muslims, Christmas for Christians, and of course, Diwali for the original inhabitants of the city.

Because of its heterogeneous population, Delhi truly embodies the spirit of India in every sense of the term. The cosmopolitan nature of the city has one very positive spin off: Delhi has its large share of festivals as various ethnic groups bring with them their own, and thus each religion has its days for celebration. Also, the North Indians have an in-built sense of joy and they need a reason to give expression to their instinctive

demands. No matter which community or religion you belong to, every Delhite gleefully accepts and adopts the others as their own! As a result, Delhi not only parties till the wee hours of every New Year's first day, but these parties are not just a dining affair. There are dance shows at clubs and pubs, and the entire populace joins in to usher in the New Year. A colonial hangover, but all Indian cities start the year with a bang!

Very soon, the cosmopolitan ethos takes over and before the winter thins out, the city is celebrating Lohri, a Punjabi festival when people sing and dance around a bonfire, eating peanuts and popcorns and also making an offering of them to the fire. No, it is not a peanut party; it is accompanied with big drinking and barbequed chicken. Valentine's Day is now a big day in the Delhi-NCR calendar; both young and old profess their love through cards, coffee, and better, large-spread dinners. As the year rolls on, the pan-Indian character of the city takes over

and we are in time for the great Indian spring festival, Holi. A festival of colours, Holi is played by all sections of society with dry colours and wet colours, accompanied by sharing sweets and savouries.

It is a kind of Juggernaut which rolls on. A regular activity to celebrate India's Independence Day is to fly kites, and this is a big event especially amongst young people. Large number of kites of different designs and shapes fill the sky, some designed on the Indian tricolour, and you can stand on a terrace and see the fierce dog fight that goes on between the kites. Once the opponent's kite is cut-off, young children run past the lanes and even by lanes to retrieve the fallen kites as a souvenir. It is fun and celebration all the way.

BOISTEROUS, COLOURFUL HOLI CELEBRATIONS WITH FREE-FLOWING LAUGHTER, LIQUOR AND MISCHIEF.

As we go past Onam and Pongal, which are the major South Indian festivals, during which people feast on all kinds of delicacies of the southern states, the big bang party starts from October which continues till the year end. Dusshera is a festival linked with Durga Puja, a 5-day long festival of Bengal but now celebrated by the people of all communities. And on the last day, people assemble at the Ram Lila grounds to see huge monstrous effigies of the demons bursting into flames (the effigies are that of Ravana, the evil king who was defeated by Lord Rama) to signify the success of good over evil. This is almost immediately followed by the Festival of Lights, Diwali, which is the most auspicious day in the Business Calendar as Lakshmi, the Goddess of Wealth, is invited to all homes which are lit up. Fire crackers are burst, candles are lit outside each door, and the city is a delightful sight. All business houses and even the Government Offices are lit up and sweet boxes are exchanged as a token of good wishes between families and business associates.

Like any part of the world, the Christmas week is when Delhi too is in the Yuletide mood, and irrespective of which religion you belong to, which ethnic group you belong to, the city is in full swing to celebrate Xmas. Be it buying cakes or dancing till early hours of the morning, Delhi has a festive look to match any other major city of the world.

ABOVE:
DUSSEHRA. THE BURNING
OF RAVANA IS SYMBOLIC
OF GOOD TRIUMPHING
OVER EVIL.

BELOW:
COLOURFUL INDEPENDENCE
DAY KITES.

THE BIGGEST CELEBRATION OF THEM ALL – 'THE GREAT DELHI WEDDING'.

While on the subject of festivals that symbolize jubilation, the weddings in Delhi are also another way to put forward the zeal and spirit of its people. A regular Punjabi wedding is a festival in itself, for the fun-loving Punjabis and other North Indians generally try to find an excuse to celebrate whenever they can. For days together, the family of the bride and the groom huddle away to plan the marriage, the women taking special dancing lessons while the men drink away to glory. It is a month-long affair with a feast happening every night. There are visits to all the major saree-stores of the city, not to forget the jewellers' also to select the trousseau. Dress designers are commissioned by the moneyed to design the bridal wear and it is fashionable even for the groom to get his wedding suit designed by a major fashion designer. The actual wedding is in itself an event, with the horse playing a key role. It is customary that the groom reaches the bride's house atop a mare in a procession with men, women and children dancing wildly on the street alongside the mare. Crackers are burst and there are special bands which are hired to provide music to add to the pageant. However, sometimes the mare, scared by the noise and gaiety, decides to gallop away from the party with the groom left to his own devices. But otherwise, Delhi weddings are merriment, exultation and lavishness personified.

DELHI LIFE 52–67

Delhi is a living–breathing–pulsating body of contradictions. Delhi's culture is an amalgam of cultures and lifestyles from all over India and, even the world. It gives Delhi a unique identity; an identity that Delhi has created with its own measured and patented mix, a heady cocktail of the best, the quirkiest and the most fascinating of all that the world has on offer.

A delightful mix of the old and new, Delhi serves up spiritually uplifting *Qawwalis* at the Jama Masjid, *Gurbanis* at Gurudwara Bangla Sahib, and the *Aartis* at Chattarpur Mandir

and other temples. It steeps you in the enchanting history of the Lodis, Tughlaqs, Mughals and the British Raj, and links you with the future with its Metro, the sci-fi shopping malls, multiplexes, IT parks and what-nots. Weddings are huge in Delhi as is the socialite page-three culture. But, it is all relaxed, laid-back and very, very intimate. It's a place where you know all about your neighbour, your city, your world. All served up with a hefty dose of the best hospitality ever found. Delhi is unique in a very unique way.

PAGE 52: THE HUSTLE-BUSTLE OF LIFE IN OLD DELHI. A QUAINT, THOUGH UNFORGIVABLY CROWDED ADDRESS OF DELHI.

From the fascinating shopping hub of Chandni Chowk, to the majestic Red Fort, the dense residential area of Dariba and the historic Jama Masjid, 'Old Delhi' can still transport one to the old-world charm of the Mughal era. The culture of the Mughals still lives on in the residences, the food and the people itself. One could say that the Urdu Bazaar section of Old Delhi, with its many Urdu publications, is the reason this language still thrives. It is here that one finds Khari Baoli, Asia's biggest spice market, and the poet Mirza Ghalib's Haveli. The Gurudwara Sis Ganj is drowned with the most intoxicating fragrance of roses, the sheer number of books at Darya Ganj's Sunday Book Bazaar, and the prices on them are sure to amaze and delight all book lovers. Old Delhi is where one can experience, in present, the life of Delhi as it was in the past.

Delhi is the cultural centre of India with artisans and craftsmen from all over India, showcasing their creative geniuses in this city. It is the centre of music – from classical to fusion – of dance, drama, paintings, sculptures, handicrafts and what- not. Delhi, in fact, has a cultural season that stretches from October to March – this is when talent comes out in droves. The various auditoriums, the State Emporia Complex, Dilli Haat, Pragati Maidan, the National School of Drama, all receive a glorious amount of patronage.

A rapidly growing interest in all forms of art among the urban populace has made Delhi quite the buzzing hub of all things arty! The city is home to some of the most prestigious and also some of the most radical art galleries of the country. One can find works of geniuses like M.F. Husain, Manjit Bawa and Anjoli Ella Menon, who enjoy an avid collector-following globally. Masters of sculpture showcase their works too, in these minimalist, aesthetic places that are a work of art in their

COLOURFUL STREET MARKETS CAN BE AN INTERESTING ADVENTURE.

own. Patrons of art in Delhi not only possess the greats, but also enthusiastically encourage new talent. Like almost anywhere in the world, originals come dear, but one is guaranteed to find the most unusual.

Dilli Haat, a fascinating food and crafts bazaar, is a shopper's paradise. The place has a rustic charm with its earthy theme and artisans straight from the farthest villages of India. The whole idea behind this paradise is to promote the folk arts and crafts, and the different regional cuisines of India. There are sixty-two stalls in the grounds, allotted to craftsmen of different states on rotation every 15 days. So every time one goes there, it's a whole new market!

Here, one can find unusual footwear made from camel

JANPATH, THE PLACE TO SHOP FOR KITSCHY TRINKETS AND CLOTHES AT BARGAIN PRICES.

skin, brassware, sandalwood and rosewood carvings, handloom items, woollen and silk items, draperies, articles made from stone, ornaments and others. Every product is unique and is a fine example of the skills of the Indian craftsmen.

Apart from these, there are several stalls where you can get to savour Indian food. The Dilli Haat has a food plaza where you can get to taste the culinary delights from the different parts of India. Food festivals are held from time to time.

There is also Janpath at Connaught Place, where one could shop for handicrafts, interesting clothes and junk jewellery. What will astound you is not only the beauty of things on offer, but also the astonishingly low prices! The norm is to bargain, bargain and then bargain some more. Right across from Janpath is the Cottage Industries Emporium, housed in a multi-level building. This government initiative has on display a host of handicrafts from all over the country. The beautiful bronze statues and miniature paintings are especially hard to resist.

Connaught Place, or CP as it is called, is unparalleled in its own way. It is not a "market", a shopping and commercial centre rolled into one, perhaps, sliced into three concentric circles, whose pillars remain to be the architectural icons of Delhi.

It is here you can buy the best brands while reliving the old-world charm in the high-ceilinged corridors. One could buy sarees from Kalpana, Uttam's or Nalli's here. Greenways have

ABOVE:
RAJASTHANI PUPPETS AND ALL KINDS OF HANDICRAFTS IMAGINABLE ARE AVAILABLE AT THE COTTAGE INDUSTRIES AND THE STATE EMPORIA.

BELOW:
COLOURFUL BANGLES AT DILLI HAAT.

been many families' choice for wedding shopping (and that includes Sonia Gandhi shopping here for Priyanka's wedding). Wenger's, the pastry shop, is still irrefutably the best Delhi has got. Apart from the high street stores, and legendary eateries like United Coffee House, the pavements have an interesting assortment on offer, from books to trinkets to Banarsi silk throws that cost as much as twenty thousand rupees!

For generations, CP has been the biggest hangout place for youngsters. Just walking around in groups, in pairs, alone. It seems the place is ageless and many new generations will flock to this piece of Delhi's history, making it their own as they pass.

Off Connaught Place, on Baba Kharak Singh Marg is the house of all Indian State Emporia. Each of them selling the best of their handicrafts, cottage crafts and textiles, covering anything and everything from furniture to dress material.

Traditionally, Delhi has been a sought-after shopping destination. In fact, it is considered a shopaholic's dream!

The shopping story should ideally have started with Chandni Chowk, Delhi's oldest and traditional market. A historical landmark in itself, it is an iconic shopping belt, and no matter what strata of the society a family belongs to, Chandni Chowk is the one and only place to shop for a marriage in the family. Be it jewellery, dresses, decorations, Chandni Chowk is a shopper's paradise. The market is divided into *katras*, which is better described as a section/segment, and there is a *katra* for each product category. The lanes known as *gullies* are also dedicated to a particular product or food, the most notable being 'Paranthewalli Gully', where all the shops serve all possible varieities of paranthas, and 'Gully Kababiyan', is famous for kebabs and biryanis. In between, the market is dotted with numerous eateries, especially *chaats* and sweets, and a day at Chandni Chowk becomes memorable for more than one reason.

THE FAMOUS KINARI BAZAAR AT CHANDNI CHOWK IS A MAJOR WEDDING SHOPPING HUB.

Khan Market just off near Lodi Gardens and Golf Course has been an elitist's stopover, and even today has been able to maintain the same positioning. People living in elite belts like Jor Bagh, Golf Links, and adjoining areas, would only buy their vegetables to music CD from Khan Market. Shopping at Khan Market is almost a lifestyle statement even if you are buying a kilo of vegetables.

Post the settlement of Punjabis in Delhi after the partition, a major market came up in Karol Bagh, and for many years, till South Delhi was developed, Karol Bagh in West Delhi was the place to be seen at. It was a general market, a more modern Chandni Chowk, and like in Chandni, the ladies would top the day with a visit to 'Roshan di Kulfi' for kachoris and of course, kulfi.

Over the years, South Delhi has been identified as the modern face of Delhi, and naturally, the Defence Colony Market had for years held the pride of place as the hang-around place, especially for eating-out, but very soon, the markets at GK-I, both M Block and N Block, started drawing the crowd. The N Block Market is famous for the original Fabindia store, and had become a destination point for people who loved ethnic wear.

Another busy market in South Delhi is at South Extension, both Part I and Part II. Some of the stores in this market, like Pall Mall and Sehgal Brothers are renowned for stocking major international brands of men's wear, like Versace and Burberry.

Delhi, a cosmopolitan shopping hub, and in fact the NCR, can boast of some of the best shopping malls of the country. The ones that are absolutely a must-visit are one – DLF Emporio – this place is heaven for those who want to shop International and Indian designer gear, with labels like Roberto Cavalli, Calvin Klein, and many, many more. The best part is the feeling of luxurious serenity... it is like shopping in the relaxed environs of a five-star lobby with no noise and fabulous service. Then,

there is the DLF Promenade which is a delightful extension of Emporio. Both malls are shopper's heaven for those who value the good things and know to spend their money on the best.

Select Citywalk Mall and Ambience Mall, are one of their kind. Citywalk delights you with live piano music, and Ambience Mall has its own Golfworks to offer! The Great India Place Mall and Metrowalk boast of amusement parks on their grounds.

A special mention of the Delhi's designer brigade here. All, and we mean all, top designers of India are based in Delhi. Tarun Tahiliani, Ritu Beri, Ritu Kumar, Ashish Soni, Suneet Varma, Rohit Bal – you name them and they are here. One can find their studios at Mehrauli, Shahpur Jat and Hauz Khas. And most of them retail from the luxury malls too.

The exclusive designer mall, Crescent, is located in Mehrauli, near the Qutub Minar. Here, you will find yourself amongst the biggest names of the fashion industry. Find 'Balance' with Rohit Bal, 'Girl Forever' (GFO) by Preeti Chandra, 'Aza', Abu-Sandeep's fascinating Lucknow work, Monisha Jaisingh's opulent embroidery and also a host of designer eateries!

Shahpur Jat is, in a way, Delhi's best kept secret... from concrete modernization that is. Flanked by the upmarket areas of Asiad Games Village and Hauz Khas, this sort of still-a-village has retained its quaint charm, and in fact, added to it in a rather unconventional way. As you take a walk through its narrow lanes, it is like coming upon one surprising treasure after another. Old, weathered houses and buildings have ensconced within them, the trendiest, and most eclectic of designer shops and boutiques that one could dream of. One finds everything from shoes and jewellery to clothes and books. It's no wonder then, that this urban village is a popular shopping haunt for the locals as well as visitors.

Santushti Shopping Complex is another place one can go for an out-of-the-world shopping experience. Set amidst lush gardens, the shops and boutiques are like lovely cottages joined together by cobbled pathways. One can shop cigars, wines, designer gear and home things here, and just lie back and relax at the refreshing Basil and Thyme Café.

Museums in Delhi contain the whole history of India within them. From the Wars of Independence, Mughal memorabilia, early scientific finds to stamps; everything is covered. There are specially dedicated museums for great personalities like Mahatma Gandhi and Mirza Ghalib. The National Police Museum is a thrilling, sensational novelty, showcasing crime and criminals from the ancient to the modern times. The National

THE FLOWER MARKET AT MEHRAULI IS A DELIGHT FOR THE SENSES.

Rail Museum still has on display the world's oldest locomotive in working condition! The Sanskriti Kendra Terracotta and Metal Museum houses what it calls 'Everyday Art', depicting the story of life. The Shankar's Doll Museum is a delight for children as well as adults with a collection of 6000 dolls from over 85 countries. The museums of Delhi present the majestic and glorious past, preserved in ancient manuscripts, specimen of beautiful art and craft, and whole lot more depicting the fascinating land that is India.

And linking it all together is The Delhi Metro. It has become a lifeline of the city, connecting most major areas and easing up the road traffic situation. It serves Delhi, Noida and Gurgaon. Its strategically-placed stations have made it surprisingly easy to travel to areas like Connaught Place, Chandni Chowk, Karol Bagh etc. – taking away the pain of parking. The stations offer ATMs, food outlets, cafes and convenience stores.

STREET FOOD STALLS OUTSIDE A METRO STATION FOR A QUICK BITE BEFORE THE COMMUTE.

OPPOSITE PAGE:
THE NEW LIFELINE OF THE CITY – THE DELHI METRO.

FOOD 68–83

4

Food is an integral part of Delhi's culture. In fact, the entire city is a huge food court. Nowhere in India do you see such a wide spread of local and international cuisine, be it the regular staple Daal Makhni[1] or Neopolitan Pastas.

The reasons are not difficult to see. The city has a perfect blend of local vegetarian dishes; the cuisine of the Muslim invaders; the influence of surrounding states; the recipes imported by the different Indian communities who moved into Delhi after it became the Capital in 1911; and subsequently, the international fare, Italian to Mexican, blended perfectly with the

---

[1] Daal Makhni: Lentils with spices cooked over slow fire in a clay pot, and topped with white butter or clarified butter (ghee) and cream. Daal or lentils, is a permanent dish in any North Indian household, either had with *rotis* (leavened bread) or *chawal* (rice). In fact, 'Daal Chawal' is a common term used to signify a meal.

upper strata and slowly, became a favourite with the upwardly mobile middle class.

The cuisine in Delhi is a combination of a range of vegetarian recipes, some based on traditional favourites of different castes who form the original inhabitants of Delhi, and a wide number of mutton and chicken dishes, many of which have been developed with Mughlai influence. For instance, there exists a Kyastha[1] cuisine, which can be considered as typical Delhi fare. It consists of Moong Daal Samosas, Bhindi (ladyfinger) Kachoris and Matar Paneer.[2] Other local favourites include Rajma Chawal, Kadi Chawal, Paneer variants and Choley Chawal. One of the best locations in Delhi to try out the local cuisine is Chandni Chowk, near Red Fort, where you can treat yourself to these dishes particularly from street-side joints.

The Chandni Chowk area, now also known as Delhi-6, is the essence of Delhi's street food, especially for *chaats*, an iconic Delhi fare of snacks. It is quite difficult to describe the meaning of *'chaat'* in one word, as there is no English equivalent. They are a range of sweet and sour savouries, crumbled potato chops

[1] Kyastha: A sub-sect of the Hindu high-caste Brahmins, whose ancient profession was writing. Some of the famous Kyasthas were Swami Vivekananda, Rishi Aurobindo, Swami Prabhupada (ISCKON) and Maharishi Mahesh Yogi. They are spread all over North India.

[2] Moong Daal Samosas: Deep-fried dumplings with lentils filling / Kachoris: Round-shaped deep-fried dumplings / Matar Paneer: Peas and cottage cheese curry

ABOVE:
RICH, AROMATIC GRAVIES ARE TYPICAL OF MUGHLAI CUISINE. DAAL OR LENTILS COOKED ON SLOW FIRE AND SPICED WITH MASALAS, AND NAAN ARE THE OFT CHOSEN ACCOMPANIMENTS WITH A DISH OF MUGHLAI MUTTON OR CHICKEN.

BELOW:
ALOO CHAAT, THAT IS, FRIED POTATOES SPICED UP WITH MASALAS AND A DASH OF LEMON, IS AN ALL-TIME FAVOURITE SNACK.

PAGE 73:
ROADSIDE SNACKS AND SAVOURIES. DELHI IS ESSENTIALLY A CHAAT CITY. FEATURED HERE IS THE ALOO TIKKI, THE BUTTER-SOAKED PAO BHAAJI AND THE MOUTHWATERING GOL GAPPAS.

केदारनाथ प्रेम चन्द हलवाई
दुकान न.4, तिराहा किनारी बाज़ार, मालीवाडा, दिल्ली-6. (फोन :- 3288557)

DILLIWALLAHS HAVE A
COMPULSIVE SWEET TOOTH AND
HALWAIS (SWEETMEAT MAKERS)
HAVE TURNED INTO FOLKLORE.
GHANTEWALLAH AT CHANDNI
CHOWK IS THE OLDEST SHOP IN
DELHI. GULAB JAMUNS, JALEBIS,
PEDAS, LADDUS ARE MOST
POPULAR, WHILE NO DIWALI
GIFT IS COMPLETE UNLESS IT
COMES WITH A BOX OF BURFIS,
EVEN IF THE MAIN GIFT CAN BE
SWAROVSKI CRYSTALS. WEDDING
INVITATIONS TOO, ARE SENT
ALONG WITH A BOX OF SWEETS.

known as *tikkis*, into a mix of curd, mint leaf & sweet tomato chutneys, and spiced with garam masalas, salt and pepper. The other *chaats* include Papri Chaats (crisp, deep-fried roundels, crumbled and mixed with sweet & sour sauces), Dahi Bhallas (fried, fluffy doughnut-shaped flour cakes with a generous helping of curd and sauces) and the ever-popular Gol Gappas, also known as Pani Puris (small, crisp pastry shells made from wheat or *suji,* filled with tamarind water). Drop by at Sitaram Bazar in the Chandni Chowk area for a *chaat* experience, ideally from a roadside stall. Some of the Pani Puri stalls also branded as "Kulkutta ishtyle" (a la Kolkata style) Phuchkas, are available with the tamarind dissolved in mineral water to add to the hygiene, but of course, they cost a little more.

The other varities of roadside delights are Pao Bhaji, a potato mixture served with bread generously fried in butter, and Fried Noodles, a Indian interpretation of chinese cuisine.

The standard breakfast in North India, be it in Delhi or adjoining areas right up to Punjab, is the Parantha, in most cases made with a filling of potatoes, cauliflower or even cottage cheese and served with curd or pickles. The North Indians are not very conscious of the calorie count, basically being agrarian in nature, and thus the paranthas are coated with dollops of butter. The other popular breakfast, also an anytime snack is Puri Bhaji, soft, deep-fried fluffy roundels, often mixed with a lentil (Bedmi Puris), served with a vegetable dish, mostly potato curry and pickles. These are standard fares and you can get

THE STREET FOOD PANORAMA – THE PERFECT OPTIONS FOR A NICE, HEAVY INDIAN BREAKFAST OR A SATIATING BITE AS YOU SHOP IN THE BAZAARS OF OLD DELHI. TAKE YOUR PICK OF PARANTHAS, PURIS OR KACHORIS, WITH JALEBIS TO SWEETEN THE DEAL AND THE NAWABI PAAN TO WRAP UP THE MEAL.

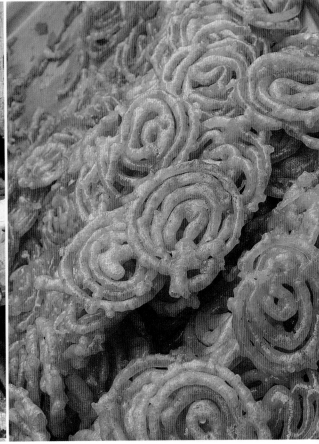

them all over the city in any Indian restaurant serving North Indian dishes. You can try the roadside carts but while their preparations are also matchless, they may not be hygienically cooked.

The Punjabi cuisine is by and large a robust meal which is spicy, rich, mostly non-vegetarian and has a generous dose of Muslim influence. Some of the all-time favourites are Chicken Butter Masala, Kadhai Chicken, Chicken Masala; a regular menu will also cover the Mughlai items like Mutton Roghan Josh, Mutton Rezala, Kheema Mutter and many such dishes that have slowly become Indian. If you are looking for a real Delhi style North Indian meal, try the food at the 'United Coffee House', also known as UCH at Connaught Place. You may also try eating at 'Punjabi by Nature', 'Chor Bizzare', and 'Moti Mahal', for a regular "pucca" Punjabi style khaana. If after a late-night session, you find that the major eateries have closed down, try and visit Pandara Road Market, which is open till late hours and order Punjabi dishes at 'Pindi', which will guarantee a finger-licking treat.

The roadside fare in Delhi is not just popular, but is economical also, and is slowly becoming a style statement for the rich. Cooked and served from a colourful cart which has the speciality spelt out in Hindi, these joints serve their own Choley Chawal, Rajma Chawal or Amritsari Naan and Subzi. They are located near all office complexes and start their service from 11 in the morning till almost 5 in the evening. You may also opt for a *Thali*, which is a set meal, comprising rice, 4 chapattis[1], one daal and one vegetable dish of the day. In all thalis or single dish

---

[1] Chapatti: Leavened bread

meals, Raita[1] is served free. The street food has now become fancy enough for the elite class, so, a few upscale eateries have modelled themselves on carts. At 'Khajja Chowk', a popular eatery in the malls, you can sit inside an auto-rickshaw and have your meal! Perhaps the rich, many of whom might have been street food customers in their struggling years, now have the pleasure of returning to their roots in airconditioned comfort without being declassed.

If you travel across Delhi-NCR, you will find 'Agarwal Sweets' boards at almost every 3 kilometres but while there may have

---

[1] Raita: a curd-based preparation in which curd is whisked with vegetables or *boondi*. A North Indian home can make many varieties of raita. It is very popular in summer as it acts as a digestive aid to an otherwise rich meal.

been an original Agarwal, they are not a chain of sweetmeat shops. Almost all sweetmeat shops in Delhi are branded as Agarwal Sweets who not only serve *mithais*, but also savouries like samosas and the likes. Another chain of sweet savoury items is 'Haldiram's', spread all over the city, many of them in fancy malls. However, for the record, the oldest shop in Delhi is 'Ghantewllah' in Chandni Chowk, which is over 150 years old. The regular sweet tooth indulges in Jalebis, at times served with rabri. 'The Bengali Sweet Shop' and 'Kaleva' at Gole Market are favourite stopovers and you can also try 'Evergreen' at Green Park market for their cashew burfis. Gurgaon, a part of Delhi-NCR, is famous for milk cakes and dhoda. 'Shyam Sweets' and 'Om Sweets' are the best choice for dhodas.

In all cities in the dry North India, non-alcoholic drinks from *sherbats* to fruit juices are very popular and are almost a part of the staple diet. The most common and popular is Lassi, simply, buttermilk. A real cooler, it is served in two options: Meethi or Namkeen. The former is the more popular sweetened

ABOVE:
DELHI IS DOTTED WITH LOCAL BAKERY AND SWEET SHOPS, AND SOME OF THE FAMOUS BRANDS ARE AGARWAL SWEETS, HALDIRAM'S AND BIKANERWALA. TRADITIONAL HALWAIS, WHO ALSO MAKE ACCOMPANYING FRIED SNACKS, HAVE ALL UPGRADED AND ARE NOW PRESENT IN MALLS, COMPETING WITH INTERNATIONAL BRANDS SUCCESSFULLY.

variation while the other is the salted version. Of course, the sweetened version is really sweet and a special lassi vendor will add a few drops of 'Rooh Afza', a very popular brand of a juice concerntrate, a few cubes of ice and top it up with a few rose petals! That is a 'Nawabi lassi' for you.

An average *Dilliwallah* is likely to have a glass of lassi at breakfast during tough summer months, and a few more during the day. A well-made lassi, using good quality curd, and well-whisked, is really a royal drink which one just can't have in one-go!

As you cut across Delhi and NCR, you will find the streets are dotted with Fruit Juice stalls. At a first look, they seem to be part of a retail chain as all fruit juice stalls virtually follow the same style of lettering, colours and the kitsch painting of a man's face drinking alongside that of a woman.

Inside the fruit juice stalls, you will notice that the fruits are stacked in the same manner and the juices are available in 3

ABOVE AND OPPOSITE PAGE, BELOW: FRUITS AND FRUIT JUICES ARE VERY POPULAR, ESPECIALLY IN THE SUMMER MONTHS. THE CITY IS FILLED WITH ROADSIDE JUICE MAKERS WHO MAKE EXOTIC JUICES LIKE MIXED FRUIT JUICE, AND CARROT JUICE SPICED WITH CORIANDER LEAVES.

sizes, Small, Medium and Large. These refer to the size of the glass, though nowadays you can get them in disposable glasses which you carry away with you, a relief from standing in front of the stall. All seasonal fruits are available, and in case you don't really have a favourite fruit, you can opt for a Mixed Fruit Juice. Of course, having a fruit cocktail is one thing, having a Mixed Fruit Juice punch is another. The flavour of all different kinds of fruits get churned together, leaving a peculiar taste as you sip the drink, hoping that a bit of goodness of all the chosen fruits will provide added enrichment to your body, and specially in the summer, to the mind.

Shikanji, a local concoction made by dissolving masalas in lemonade, served with ice is a very popular cooler, from street-side fare to the pubs.

While North India has been high on the alcohol quotient, with whiskey being the major liquor sold. Delhi, in the ninetees had a very few limited drinking holes and most of them were located in hotel coffee shops and bars. The first such "pub-like"

CONNAUGHT PLACE – A PLACE TO SHOP, EAT, TAKE-IN THE CULTURE OF DELHI OR JUST BE. THE WHITE PILLARED CORRIDORS ARE ODDLY CALMING EVEN WITH A LARGE NUMBER OF PEOPLE PASSING THROUGH THEM.

feel came when 'Rodeo' opened the first Tex-Mex eatery in Connaught Place. The fare was probably a bit before its time as the kebab and curry eating Delhite took some time to adjust to Enchilladas and Quesidillas (and a Tequilla shot) but the saddle-topped bar stools did give the sporting types a Western feel. A few years ago the state government relaxed their rules relating to bars and pubs, and soon the city had a spate of pubs which seemed to mushroom out of nowhere. The opening of the pubs seemed to have been timed with the growing rich who had a lot of money to spend, thanks mainly to the liberalisied economic policies and as a result, a special brand of "pub and lounge" culture got added to the city's nightlife. While a large number of them have shut down, the more popular ones remain, and all bars & pubs have a great weekdays offer of 'Happy Hours' where you can buy one drink and get one free. If you are looking for a quiet place to go guzzle some beer on a hot afternoon, you can try the 'Knight Lounge' near Plaza cinema or the good old 'Rodeo', just above the 'KFC' in Connaught Place. The most fashionable place to visit is, of course, 'Olive Bar & Kitchen' in Mehrauli.

A recent addition to the Delhi's flavour is Wine. The ease of availability, growth in international travels and the efforts of Subhash Arora of Indian Wine Academy, have made many to switch to wines; and equally important is the consumers' knowledge about different types of wine, wine drinking and wine habits.

If Rodeo is the Tex-Mex joint, Delhi also offers a host of international cuisine eateries. Italian, Japanese, Lebanese, Korean, Frontier delights, Sizzlers, Steaks, Tepanyaki; all kinds of food and all types of dishes. Fast-food joints like 'McDonald's' and 'KFC', and international chains like 'Ruby Tuesday', 'Pizza

THE PUB CULTURE HAS BEEN A NEW DEFINITION OF LIFESTYLE OVER THE PAST FEW YEARS.

Hut' and 'TGIF' are fully operative in Delhi-NCR, and almost anytime and anywhere you can dig into a burger or a pasta. To that, you add the speciality Indian cuisine outlets; so be it a Bengali fish and rice lunch or a Malayalee appam and stew breakfast, the city is packed with the best that country has to offer. Steamed dumplings, or Momos are a very popular North-Eastern anytime snack in this region.

One way of trying the speciality dishes of all Indian states is to visit the various State Guest Houses in the city as all the Indian states like West Bengal, Tamil Nadu have their own buildings which serve as a Delhi Office and also as a Transit point for people visiting Delhi, and all of them run a catering service which is open to public. So, if you are looking for an authentic Chennai lunch spread, do visit the 'Tamil Nadu Bhawan' or for a hot and spicy Chicken Rice lunch (which will leave you sweating), try the 'Andhra Bhawan'. Those of you who are fond of fish try the 'Utkal Bhawan' or 'Banga Bhawan' or 'Asom Bhawan' as they churn out Oriya, Bengali and Assamese

INTERNATIONAL BRANDS LIKE MCDONALD'S AND KFC HAVE CAUGHT THE IMAGINATION OF THE YOUTH AND AGED ALIKE. BURGERS, PIZZAS AND FRIED CHICKEN ARE VERY POPULAR AND HAVE ALMOST BECOME A PART OF THE LOCAL CUISINE.

style of fish dishes.

If you have a few hours in hand, do drop in at 'Dilli Haat', a handicraft and food court opposite the INA market, where almost each state from India has a food stall. You can check out Radhaballavis with Alur Dom in the Bengal stall, Pao Bhaji at the Maharashtra stall, Avadhi Biriyani at the Uttar Pradesh stall, and most certainly, Wazwan dishes washed down with Kahwah at the Kashmir stall.

Finally, if you were to ask which are the "must-visits" in Delhi, the first choice would undoubtedly be 'Karim's' at Jama Masjid for Biryani and Kebabs. And yes, the Tandoori Chicken is a delicacy at 'Moti Mahal', Darya Ganj. Order Naans and a Daal to go with it. 'Karim's' is of course an institution, almost a Delhi icon, and an essential stopover to experience the city's heritage.

The five-star hotels of Delhi have some of the best restaurants serving delightfully scrumptious food with great ambience and a presentation to die for. They also boast the best 24-hour coffee shops, and also the finest bakeries in the city.

Delhi is now also home to some of the best café chains. 'Barista Lavazza', 'Café Coffee Day', 'Costa Coffee' and 'The Coffee Bean & Tea Leaf' are the lifeline of the young crowd, and also for those who value a good cuppa!

MOMOS, OR STEAMED DUMPLINGS, A TIBETAN DELICACY, HAS ATTAINED HUGE POPULARITY IN THE PAST FEW YEARS. ONE-MAN MOMO SELLERS ARE DOING BRISK BUSINESS WITH THIS NEW-FOUND ANYTIME SNACK.

SPORTING DELHI **84–89**

In the epic Mahabharata, Bheem, the third Pandava brother was gifted with enormous strength and was an expert wrestler. Throughout the story, he wrestles his way to victory, ultimately killing his cousin, Duryodhan, who symbolizes evil, in a wrestling match. Mahabharata is full of drama and graphic descriptions, and is quite gruesome with incidents like Bheem keeping his promise to Draupadi to avenge her insult at the hand of Kauravas. He kills Dushasana, tearing his chest, drinking the blood oozing from his body, and smearing himself with the same, and also wounding Duryodhan with a foul blow below the waist in the Kurukshetra War.

The tradition of wrestling, Indian style, colloquially called *kushti* continues to be a popular sport in India and Pakistan.

Delhi is no exception and the entire Delhi-NCR is dotted with *akharas*, which are traditional rings where wrestlers grapple with each other. The rings are no fancy WWF stages. They are sand wrestling pits, which are used for training and competition. The wrestlers are called *pehalwans* and even today it continues to be a popular sport with a sizeable following.

While wrestling continues to be the traditional sport, Delhi had its first taste of hosting an international event in 1951, when it hosted the first Asian Games. It must have been an uphill task for a new nation to organize a multi-sport event, and as a result they were successful in sowing the seeds of friendship amongst the Asian countries.

In 1982, the city was host to another Asiad; and this time around, the city saw a huge infrastructural development and development of modern stadia.

In between the two Asiads, there were other sporting developments. One was the Durand Trophy, which though initiated in 1880 in Shimla, had been shifted to Delhi in 1940, and was a feast for soccer lovers of the city. One of the premier football tournaments in India, the Durand, has now become a major national event with all the media razzmatazz that is so much a part of the sporting extravaganzas.

If the current crop of international cricketers has more than one player from Delhi pitching for the best in category, the answer lies in the development of Feroz Shah Kotla Cricket Stadium, which is the game arena for the Delhi Daredevils. The game of cricket, like elsewhere in the country, is a religion that brings all sections of people together. The ground, which boasts great test matches (where Mansur Ali Khan, Nawab of Pataudi, made his debut, and Anil Kumble had taken his record 10 wickets in an innings) has been a permanent venue for all cricketing

A VIEW OF THE
DELHI GOLF COURSE.

OPPOSITE PAGE,
ABOVE:
A PACK OF POLO PLAYERS
OF THE NATIONAL TEAM,
CHARGING IN HOT PURSUIT.
BELOW:
CELEBRATIONS ANNOUNCING
THE MASCOT OF 'THE
COMMONWEALTH GAMES
2010, SHERA.

events and now has a world-class stadium to add to its feathers. The Delhi team, which has Virendrer Sehwag, Gautam Gambhir, Ashish Nehra, Amit Mishra and Ishant Sharma in their ranks, has emerged as one of the key teams in the domestic Ranji Trophy tournament, having won it six times since its inception.

Amidst such popular games like cricket and football, the game that seems to have caught the imagination of the new generation is Golf. The city is full of golfers, not just the forty-plus men and women swinging the club, but youngsters too have been flocking to the numerous golf courses across NCR. It is not just a lifestyle statement, but with opportunities opening up, a large number of players from Delhi and North India have turned pros in the international circuit. Though still in the

elitist domain, with Arnold Palmer and Jack Nicklaus signature courses, the pride of place goes to the Delhi Golf Club. At once exclusive, it is a Club with a rich history and has been able to manage the rich golfing tradition with changing times.

The other very elitist sport in the city is the game of Polo. Come winter and you have the people who matter, the glitterati, ex-Royalty, all making a fashion statement under the sun.

And now, the Commonwealth Games of 2010. Not just the stadia and the related infrastructure, but the entire city and the people are gearing up to make it an event to remember. For every one who lives in Delhi-NCR, it is a personal affair, and the management bodies too, are extending themselves to provide the visitors a memorable time in Delhi.

RELIGION 90–105

6

LEFT:
LORD GANESHA, FAVOURITE
GOD OF THE HINDUS. HE
IS THE GOD OF AUSPICIOUS
BEGINNINGS.

RIGHT:
KARMAPA INTERNATIONAL
BUDDHIST INSTITUTE

PAGE 90:
GOD IS OMNIPRESENT;
HE'S EVEN THERE IN THE
MUNDANE – BLESSING THE
RICKSHAW!

While the city of Delhi may not be a religious destination, the city has people from all faiths living in harmony, sharing the joys and joining in the celebration of each other's faith. The Hindus, the original inhabitants of the city, are the largest in number, and the city is dotted with temples, some major ones dedicated to Lord Hanuman, the popular Monkey-God, who was believed to have helped Lord Rama in his battle against the evil Ravana. The city also has huge statues of Lord Shiva, who is known as the "destroyer of evil", and there are numerous ancient Shiva temples, tucked away in the green belt. Monkeys are respected, fed and at times chased away, when they descend in numbers causing havoc in residential areas. Goddess Durga, the powerful mother, is a favourite amongst North Indians, as are Lakshmi

and Ganesha, who are worshipped jointly during Diwali with the hope of bringing prosperity.

Over the years, people in North India have caught on to the traditional Hindu/Buddhist systems of living by adopting *Vaastu* system of positioning and lifestyle. Delhi was also the epicentre of the great Hindu epic, The Mahabharata. The battle between the Kauravas and the Pandavas during which Lord Krishna sermonized the master-archer Arjuna, took place at Kurukshetra, which is just 100 kms away.

The Buddhists were also perhaps one of the early visitors to the city as Delhi was a stopover in the ancient times, being en route Taxila from Magadha (current-day Bihar). However, today majority of Buddhists are the new-generation Tibetans, whose

LEFT:
GODDESS DURGA, DESTROYER OF EVIL, IS WORSHIPPED AND CELEBRATED WITH GREAT FERVOUR DURING THE NINE-DAY DURGA PUJA FESTIVAL.

RIGHT:
THIS MAGNIFICENT STATUE OF LORD HANUMAN WAS MANY YEARS IN THE MAKING, AND FORMS THE ENTRANCE TO A TEMPLE.

A PEACEFUL QUIET MARKS THE SERENE LOTUS TEMPLE.

ancestors were driven out by the Chinese, or they had escaped along with The Dalai Lama. Delhi-NCR has a huge following of Ikeda, the new-generation Japanese philosopher.

Delhi has some remarkable temples, amongst which is the 'Birla Mandir'. Built in 1938 by Raja Baldeo Das Birla, who founded India's biggest business family, the temple has long been a landmark of Delhi. It is dedicated to Goddess Lakshmi, who is worshipped for wealth, and Lord Vishnu, one of the Gods of the Holy Hindu triumvirate supposed to preserve the earth and by appearing to this mortal world in various incarnations, one of them being Rama. The temple was inaugurated by Mahatma Gandhi who had laid down the condition that people of all caste and creed would be allowed to worship, and till date, this is being maintained.

'The Lotus Temple', standing amidst lush green lawns is the Baha'i Temple with 27 white marble petals, shaped into a lotus, and so it is also known as the "Lotus Temple". Made of white marble, it is considered a modern-day architectural marvel. This 40 metre high temple is the seventh Baha'i[1] place of worship in India.

Another magnificent temple complex worth a mention is the 'Chattarpur Temple Complex'. A few kilometers down the Qutub complex, is the Chattarpur Temple Complex. There are a series of huge Hindu temples on either side of the road. Though these are modern-day temples, they are beautiful and architectural marvels. The main temple is devoted to Goddess Durga, though there are temples devoted to all other major Gods in the Hindu pantheon (which has 33 crore divinities!).

---

[1] The members of Baha'i Faith are followers of Bahaullah and its members are spread over 200 countries. The Baha'i followers believe in the Unity of God, Religion and Humankind.

THE BIRLA TEMPLE THAT WAS
INAUGURATED BY MAHATMA
GANDHI ON THE CONDITION
THAT PEOPLE OF ALL FAITHS BE
ALLOWED TO ENTER IT.

OPPOSITE PAGE,
ABOVE:
CHATTARPUR MANDIR IN
ALL ITS GRANDEUR.
BELOW, LEFT:
LORD SHIVA OF THE HOLY
TRIUMVIRATE IS THE
DESTROYER OF ALL EVILS.
BELOW, RIGHT:
A TEMPLE THROUGH THE
CAVERNOUS MOUTH OF A
VANQUISHED DEMON, WHO LIES
AT THE FEET OF LORD HANUMAN.

The 'Digambar Jain Temple' is the oldest Jain temple, originally built in 1526. Also known as Lal Mandir, it is located at the entrance of Chandni Chowk, opposite the Red Fort. The main deity of the temple is Lord Mahavira who, many believe, is the founder of Jainism.

The whole of Delhi also has millions of 'Prachin Shiva Mandirs', which means ancient temples devoted to Lord Shiva. Many of them are in the parks and forests, but these are non-descript temples set up for commercial purposes. It is unlikely that such ancient temples had been installed in the city of Delhi alone.

A latest addition to the list of temples in Delhi is 'Akshardham'. Also known as 'Swaminarayan[1] Akshardham', it

[1] Also known as Sahajanand Swami, founder of Swaminarayan Faith, a form of Vaishnavism. The Hindu sect is believed to have almost 20 million followers.

is believed to draw almost 75% of tourists visiting Delhi. Built under the supervision of Bochanwasi Shri Akshar Purushottam Swaminarayan Sanstha by 3000 artisans, the temple is located on the banks of Yamuna, close to the Commonwealth Games Village. Crafted entirely out of stone, the temple also has an IMAX feature on the history of India.

The oldest temple in Delhi and perhaps India is believed to be the 'Kalkaji Temple', which drew visitors from the characters in the Mahabharata (3000 years ago). This temple was razed to the ground by Mughal invaders. Devoted to Goddess Kali, hence the name 'Kalkaji', it was later repaired by Raja Kedarnath, treasurer of Akbar II in the mid-nineteenth century.

The ancient 'Hanuman Mandir', located in Connaught Place of Delhi, has a magnificent tale to its origin and historical presence. It is believed that this temple, built in honour of the Hindu deity Hanuman, was constructed by the Pandava brothers, at the time of the Mahabharata. One of the most notable structures of the temple is the presence of an Islamic

crescent moon at the spire of the temple, therefore making the temple immortal even during the phase of religious destruction during the reign of Islamic dynasties and invaders.

According to the Mahabharata, the second Pandava brother, Bheem was theologically the brother of Hanuman, both being sons of the Wind God, Pawan. As per the tale of the Mahabharata, when the Pandavas returned to the throne of Indraprastha after their thirteen year exile, they built five temples to honour five Hindu deities, and the Hanuman Mandir was also one of them.

Much later, during the reign of either Humayun or Akbar, it was believed that the epic poet, Tulsidas had been asked to perform a miracle at the Hanuman Mandir by the Mughal Emperor. With the help of Hanuman himself, Tulsidas was able to please the Emperor who, as a sign of gratitude, placed that Islamic crescent moon on the Mandir's structure.

The Hanuman Temple still remains one of the most popular religious locations on the map of Delhi, with the famous 24-hour chanting of the hymn, "Sri Ram, Jai Ram, Jai Jai Ram", which has been in motion since the 1st of August, 1964. This act is mentioned in the Guinness Book of World Records.

With the advent of Mohammad Ghori in the 12th century, the city started receiving the chunk of Muslim warriors, and for the next 800 years, the city was ruled by one Muslim dynasty or the other. The city boasts one of the biggest mosques in the world, the 'Jama Masjid', built by Mughal emperor Shah Jahan. Though an unfortunate decision in history led to the partition of India in 1947, with many old-time Muslims opting to go over to Pakistan, the city lives in complete harmony still, with respect for Muslims and their places of religion. During the month of Ramzan, hosting of Iftar parties is a regular affair; it does not

matter if the host is a Hindu. It is a way of sharing each other's faith and bringing together of a great nation called India.

The 'Nizamuddin Dargah', located just across Humayun's Tomb, the shrine of Sufi Saint Nizamuddin Auliya, attracts visitors from Muslims and Hindus alike. Built by Mohammad Bin Tughlaq, who was devoted to Saint Nizamuddin, the shrine also houses the tombs of Amir Khasrau, famous poet and disciple of Nizamuddin, poet Mirza Ghalib and Jahan Ara, Shah Jahan's daughter. Nizamuddin died in 1325 and the present tomb was built in 1562.

Another famous Masjid is the 'Masjid Moth' or 'Moth-ki-Masjid', located behind South Extension II in South Delhi. Over 500 years old, it was built by one Miyan Bhuwa, a minister in the Court of Sikandar Lodi. The story goes that Sikandar Lodi used to give a reward of one grain of lentil, known as *Moth*, the Hindustani word for lentil. Miyan planted the seed, and overtime, they multiplied to provide him with the funds to build the mosque. It is a small mosque, devoid of minarets or calligraphic designs.

Other famous masjids/dargahs in Delhi are Chiragh I Dilli Dargah, Mosque of Makhdum Sabzwari, Gumbad Masjid, Khirkee Masjid, and Fatehpuri Masjid amongst others.

A large number of people in Delhi are also followers of Sufism, a moderate form of Islam where expressing devotion to the God is through singing and dancing.

The period of Muslim occupation also saw the rise of the brave Sikh race and since traditionally Punjab, the state of the Sikhs, is just next to Delhi, the city has been witness to many historical events concerning the Sikhs, including the tragic beheading of the Sikh Guru, Tegh Bahadur. Today, there is a sizeable number of Sikhs in Delhi, and some of the finest Gurudwaras are located in the city. The Sikhs are highly disciplined; they compulsorily take to social services as a means of practicing religion, and being casteless in nature, the Gurudwaras are always open to people from any faith. In the main Hindu religion, fighting the strife and the curse of the deplorable caste system, the philosophy of the Sikhs is bliss!

Delhi is surrounded by eminent Gurudwaras. During the reign of Sikandar Lodi, a Muslim sage used to ferry people across the Yamuna. He wanted to meet God, and so people called him 'Majnu'. In the 15th century, Guru Nanak, founder of Sikhism, came and lived near Majnu's abode, and with the blessings of Guru Nanak, Majnu attained enlightenment. He became his follower and the place came to be known as 'Majnu

THE OUTSIDE VIEW OF THE GURUDWARA RAKAB GANJ SAHIB, WHICH IS SURROUNDED BY A BEAUTIFUL GARDEN.

ka Tila', where a shrine was built. What was a small structure was expanded in 1980s, and a white marble structure stands today, known as 'Gurudwara Majnu ka Tila'.

'Gurudwara Sis Ganj' is linked with the martyrdom of Sikh Guru Tegh Bahadur[1], who was beheaded by Mughal emperor Aurangzeb for refusing to convert to Islam. After he was killed, there were no takers for his torso and body, till legend goes, there was a heavy downpour and two of his disciples fled with the body. It is believed that the head was taken to Chakk Nanaki in Anandpur Sahib District of Punjab, and the body to 'Gurudwara Rakab Ganj' in Delhi.

---

[1] Guru Tegh Bahadur (1621-1675) became the ninth Sikh Guru in 1655, and was killed by Aurangzeb, for refusing to convert to Islam.

The Gurudwara, known as 'Sis Ganj Sahib' comes from the word *Sis*, which means the Head. It was built by Baba Baghel Singh, a devotee of Guru Tegh Bahadur, and has in its premises, the tree trunk under which Guru Tegh Bahadur was beheaded.

When the loyal devotees of Guru Tegh Bahadur escaped with his body, it was taken to the house of Lakhi Singh and the whole house was set on fire to cremate the body and destroy the evidence. A Gurudwara was built on the site in 1732, which is very close to the Parliament House and is surrounded by gardens. The magnificent white building has prominent domes and can be visited by people of all caste and creed.

The 'Gurudwara Bangla Sahib' is located near Connaught Place. Built in 1783 by Sardar Bhagel Singh, it serves as homage to the eighth Sikh Guru, Guru Har Krishan, who had resided at that location in 1664.

It is believed that when Guru Har Krishan stayed in what was then a bungalow that belonged to Raja Jai Singh, an Indian ruler of the 17th century, there was an epidemic of small box and cholera in the city of Delhi. Guru Har Krishan had used the water from a well located at the grounds and had helped cure many sufferers. However, he contracted the disease during his endeavours and soon died himself. Raja Jai Singh went on to construct a small tank over that well and today that serves as the tank in Gurudwara Bangla Sahib, which is revered by the Sikhs as having healing properties and is therefore known as *amrit* (nectar).

Gurudwara Bangla Sahib is a congregational point for the anniversary of Guru Har Krishan, and also for the death anniversary of Maharaja Ranjit Singh.

The Gurudwara Bangla Sahib is uniquely recognized by its striking golden dome and also by its tall flagpole, which is known as the 'Nishan Sahib'.

SITAUTED IN THE CHANDNI CHOWK AREA OF OLD DELHI. THE GURUDWARA SIS GANJ SAHIB, DEFINITELY OFFERS A BREAK FROM THE CROWD OF DELHI.

CHURCH OF THE SACRED
HEART. A FASCINATING
RELIGIOUS BUILDING,
OCCUPIES A SPECIAL PLACE
IN THE HEART OF DELHI'S
CHRISTIANS.

Other major Gurudwaras are Gurudwara Nanak Piao and Pahadiwala Gurudwara.

With the advent of Englishmen came the religion of Christianity. As the East India Company grew, their cantonments and administrative services started spreading; the number of missionaries and churches grew. As in all parts of the country, the missionaries helped the Indian with education and knowledge, and all around Delhi are some of the exotic churches, some in regular service for over hundred years. With people from all over India moving in after 1947, all branches of Christianity are in practice in the city, not just Catholics and Protestants, but Syrian Christians and other similar churches.

'St James Church' is the oldest Church in Delhi built before the Mutiny. It was damaged during the Mutiny, but subsequently repaired in 1865. The Church is associated with the famous Col James Skinner who had raised the famed Skinner's Horses, and is also known as 'Skinner's Church'. Skinner built the Church at a personal cost of Ninety-five thousand rupees, and the Church was designed by Major Robert Smith. It was consecrated in 1836. Skinner, who died in 1841, was buried in the Church itself. The Church has porticoes, porches with an octagonal dome in the centre. The Church is closed on Sundays.

'Cathedral Church of Redemption' and the 'Church of Sacred Heart', both built in the 1930s, have a common architect, Henry Alexander Nesbitt Medd. Medd was a British architect and joined the team of Sir Edwin Lutyens and Sir Herbert Baker, both of whom built the Government Offices and Bungalows in New Delhi. It is shaped like a birthday cake. The Church has a tinted glass window adding to the beauty of the Church, and it is also known as the Viceroy's Church. In 1929, Lord Irwin, the then Viceroy of India, had a close shave when his train was blown up and as a token of thanksgiving, donated a Silver Cross and an organ to the Church. 'The Cathedral of Sacred Heart' is located near Gol Dak Khana, close to Connaught Place. Built on 14 acres of land, it is a Catholic Church which was initiated by Father Luke, who belonged to the Franciscan First Order. The architecture has an Italian influence with lavish interiors.

The city also has a very small population of Jews, though it is believed that they have been the inhabitants of Delhi for over 2000 years. It is a close-knit population which practices all Jewish rites at the synagogue.

ONE OF THE OLDEST CHURCHES IN DELHI, ST. JAMES' CHURCH, HAS RENAISSANCE STYLE ARCHITECTURE WITH A CENTRAL OCTAGONAL DOME.

DELHI MONUMENTS

QUTUB MINAR

The Qutub Minar is perhaps the most identifiable monument associated with Delhi. Measuring 234 meters, it is the tallest tower in the world, higher than the Leaning Tower of Pisa.

The first storey was built by Qutub-ud-din in 1202 AD, and then Iltutmish, slave and son-in-law of Qutub-ud-din who succeeded him, went on to build the second, third and fourth storey in 1231.

In 1368, the tower was struck by an earthquake which caused extensive damage to the fourth storey. By then the Tughlaqs had taken over Delhi and Firoz Khan Tughlaq (1352 – 1388) repaired the damages and replaced the fourth storey with two storeys with extensive use of marble and sandstone. He also added a cupola, which subsequently fell off, again due to an earthquake in 1803.

While the Qutub has its prototype in Ghazni, there is a view that a Hindu tower was in existence when Qutub-ud-din raised the present Minar. There is an unfinished Minar near the Qutub which was started by Alauddin Khilji (1296 – 1316), called the 'Alai Minar' as Khilji wanted to build another monument to glorify his Deccan conquests, but he died before the first storey could be completed.

IRON PILLAR

Inside the Qutub complex is the famous Iron Pillar, certainly a wonder. The pillar is perhaps a standard erected in the memory of Chandragupta II (375-413), the Maurya king. It is believed that it was a part of a Vishnu[1] Temple and a hole at the top of the pillar may have been the base for an image of Garuda, the vehicle of Vishnu. The huge pillar, which was brought to Delhi by Tomar King Anangpal, is made of pure iron which has survived any rusting.

There is a belief that if any one can grip the pillar with their back to it and make both hands meet behind it, the person's wish is fulfilled.

QUWWAT-UL-ISLAM MOSQUE

Another historical monument in the Qutub Complex is the Quwwat-ul-Islam Mosque.

Quwwat-ul-Islam, meaning 'the Might of Islam' was built with the pillars of destroyed temples. However, the use of Hindu craftsmen and recycled designs and materials of 27 demolished temples

---

[1] Lord Vushnu, part of the Holy Trinity of the Hindus, the others being Brahma and Maheshwar.

gave the mosque an un- Islamic look. The construction work started in 1192 and the prayer hall was extended during the reign of Iltutmish and subsequently, Alauddin Khilji made some additions to the mosque.

HAUZ SHAMSI

Built by Iltutmish in 1230, Hauz Shamsi is a tank. The story goes that the prophet came to Iltutmish in his dream and pointed out the site of the tank. Every year a secular festival called *Phool Walon ki Sair* begins from this site.

BALBAN'S TOMB

The tomb, which was discovered in the mid 20th century, is of historical importance as it features the true arch for the first time in India. It is also believed that it also featured the first true dome in India which however, has not survived.

SULTAN GHARI'S TOMB

Located in West Mehrauli, the tomb was built by Iltutmish in 1231 for his eldest son, Nasir-ud-din and is considered one of the oldest Muslim tombs in India. Material from destroyed Hindu temples was also used to build this tomb and even today, both Hindus and Muslims worship at this tomb.

CHOR MINAR

This Khilji monument is a tower with a lot of small, circular holes on the outside. It is believed that the holes were used to either display the heads of thieves (hence *Chor*) or the massacred heads of inhabitants of a Mongol Colony around the tower.

HAUZ KHAS COMPLEX

The Hauz Khas or the Royal Tank was built by Alauddin Khilji to supply water to his newly-built Siri Fort. However, subsequent developments of Hauz Khas were done by the Tughlaqs, who succeeded the Khiljis and the Lodis.

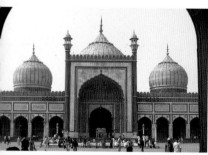

The Hauz Khas complex now has a *madrassa*, an institution of Islamic learning, and the tomb of Firoz Shah Tughlaq.

FIROZ SHAH'S TOMB

Firoz Shah's tomb (d. 1398 AD), typically Tughlaq in style with soli-looking sloping style, is at the corner of the Madrassa building. He is buried there with his son and grandson. The tomb was repaired by Sikandar Lodi in 1507 AD.

The buildings at Hauz Khas have a good degree of Hindu motifs, like lotus flowers and doorways supported by square pillars.

ALAI DARWAZA

The Alai Darwaza is actually a part of the Quwwait-ul-Islam mosque. Built around 1311 AD, it remained incomplete due to Alauddin Khilji's death. It was the Southern gate of Quwwat-ul-Islam mosque, which was enlarged by Alauddin Khilji. You can see this gate as you enter the Qutub complex.

BEGUMPUR MASJID

The Begumpur Masjid was perhaps built by Mohammad Tughlaq when he was building Jahanpanah and may have been built as the mosque of the new city. It is an impressive structure with a huge courtyard. It was perhaps the biggest mosque in Delhi till Shah Jahan built the Jama Masjid. With its imposing black domes and high walls, it gives the feel of a fort rather than a place of worship.

BIJAY MANDAL

Near the Begumpur Masjid is Bijay Mandal, which too was a part of Jahanpanah. It was perhaps the spot from where Mohammad conducted the administration of his empire. It is an octagonal tower from which you take a look around the area.

THE ASHOKA PILLAR

It was originally erected by Emperor Ashoka in Ambala in 250 BC and discovered by Firoz Shah

during a hunting expedition in 1367. It took him hundreds of men and a 42 wheeled carriage to cart it back to Delhi, wrapped in silk. The pillar is 14 meters tall, made of polished sandstone.

JAMA MASJID, FIROZ SHAH KOTLA

The Jama Masjid at Firoz Shah Kotla inspired Taimur Lang to carry back to Samarkhand most of the skilled stone masons, and it was here that he was presented with two 74 year old white parrots, which too, he took back to Samarkhand.

MUBARAK SHAH'S TOMB

This is an octagonal tomb and is located in the village of Mubarakpur. It is known as a stunted tomb.

MOHAMMAD SHAH'S TOMB

This tomb of the third Sayyid ruler who died in 1444 is also an octagonal tomb with a dome and has a verandah with pillars. The painting on the dome has a geometrical design.

HUMAYUN'S TOMB

Located in Nizamuddin (East) in New Delhi, Humayun's tomb is located right next to the Purana Qila, a citadel founded by Humayun in 1533. It was while responding to the call of evening prayers that Humayun slipped on the stairs leading out of the library he was in at the Purana Qila, and that consequently led to his death. Humayun's Tomb was declared a UNESCO World Heritage Site in 1993 and has been undergoing restoration work till date.

However, a visit to Humayun's tomb will reveal that besides the great emperor's it also houses the graves of Hamida Begum (his wife), Dara Shikoh (Mughal Emperor Aurangzeb's son) and a host of other Mughal emperor's graves over time – like Jahandar Shah, Farrukhsiyar (the Mughal emperor who actually allowed the British East India Company to trade in India), Rafi-ul-darjat and Alamgir II. Humayun's tomb played a major role in the Sepoy Mutiny of 1857, because it was the basement of the tomb that the octogenarian Mughal emperor, Bahadur Shah Zafar used as a hide-out to escape the British forces. However, he was captured from this very Humayun's tomb after being betrayed by his own people and was thereafter exiled to Rangoon where he soon died.

RED FORT

Through the years and years that it has existed, the Red Fort, also known as the 'Lal Qila' in Urdu, has become synonymous as the "pride of India" and naturally, of Delhi as well. Built in the 17th century, by the Mughal emperor, Shah Jahan, the Red Fort is basically a fort complex, in what was then considered to be the walled city of Old Delhi. It was from the Red Fort that the Mughals carried forth their royal duties, with it acting as the fort and the capital of the Mughals. The Red Fort has stood the test of time, being the capital fortress of the Mughal reign, right until the decline of the Mughal Dynasty in 1857 with the imprisonment of Bahadur Shah Zafar after the failed Sepoy Mutiny, to being the exact location where Pandit Jawaharlal Nehru hoisted the national flag when India gained independence from the British.

Construction of the Fort began in 1638, and it took ten years for the structure to be completed. The name given to the structure in 1648, by its patron and architect was "Qila-i-Mubarak", meaning "the blessed fort", as it was the residence of the royal family. The Red Fort belongs to the city Shahjahanabad in Delhi, one of the seven cities that comprise the capital. The Yamuna river which surrounds the Red Fort fed the moats that run around the structure.

Currently, this UNESCO World Heritage Site is in use every 15th August, India's Independence Day, when the national flag flies atop the Lahori Gate of the complex.

JAMA MASJID

With the construction of the Red Fort in Shajahanabad, the Mughal emperor Shah Jahan realized that they also needed a mosque in the city where people could offer prayers. The brilliant architect that he was, he started the construction of a mosque right next to the Red Fort, which was completed in 1656. The Masjid-i Jahan Numa, otherwise meaning "World-reflecting Mosque" over time came to be known as the Jama Masjid.

It took nearly 5000 workers to complete the gargantuan structure over 6 years, at an estimated cost of 1 million at that time. With three flights of steps moving towards the courtyard from the east, north and the south, the imposing structure of the Jama Masjid consists of three great gates, four towers and two 40 m high minarets made up of strips of red sandstone and white marble.

The Jama Masjid is considered to have been a replica of the Jama Masjid in Fatehpur Sikri in Agra, only that it is much larger and far more imposing than its predecessor.

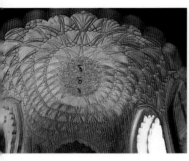

RASHTRAPATI BHAWAN

Located near the heart of Lutyen's Delhi on a small plateau, is the Rashtrapati Bhawan, or the Presidential Palace, which acts as the official residence of the Indian Head of State, or in this case, the President of India. Construction of the Rashtrapati Bhawan started in 1912, after King George V declared the change of capital from Calcutta to Delhi. Edwin Landseer Lutyen started to work on what would be the Viceroy's House in the state capital. Based heavily on Mughal and European architectural elements, the Rashtrapati Bhawan comprises of 355 decorated rooms and has a floor area of about 200,000 square feet. With the dome of the structure being inspired from the structure of the Pantheon in Rome, the Rashtrapati Bhawan is till date the largest residence of any Head of State in the whole world.

INDIA GATE

After World War I, it was decided by the British Government in India that a monument needed to be constructed, which would pay homage to the soldiers who had laid down their lives for the British Raj in the World War and also in the Third Anglo–Afghan War of 1919. Sir Edwin Lutyens was once again called upon and he constructed the 42 meter tall structure made up of red sandstone and granite. It was then known as the All India War Memorial and later on came to be known by its current name, India Gate.

After independence from British Rule, the Indian Army placed a marble cenotaph with a rifle placed on its barrel, and is crested by a soldier's helmet – known as the *Amar Jawan Jyoti*, the Indian Army's own tribute to their KIA soldiers. It was placed there in 1971. The India Gate is a national monument of India.

TEEN MURTI BHAWAN

By 1930, the British government in India deemed it fit to have designated residential quarters for the Commander-in-Chief of the British Indian Defence Forces. Therefore, the architect who had earlier been entrusted with the construction of Connaught Place, Robert Tor Russel, was asked to build a suitable structure for the supreme commander of the British Indian Armed Forces. Consequently, the Commander-in-Chief's residence was constructed over a wide expanse of area.

However, after Independence, it was deemed fit by the new Government of India to re-designate the Commander-in-Chief's residence as the official residence of the first Prime Minister of India (at that time it was just meant to be the official residence of the Prime Minister(s) of India), Pandit Jawaharlal Nehru.

However, in honour of Nehru's memory, after his death in 1964, the Prime Minister's official residence was turned into the center of contemporary studies, the headquarters of the Jawaharlal Nehru Fund, Nehru Memorial Library and also the Nehru Fellowship.

On these grounds, there stands one of the four Nehru planetariums in India, which still holds shows in its sky theater everyday at 1130 and 1500 hours. It was inaugurated by the then Prime Minister of India, Mrs Indira Gandhi in 1984. Mrs Indira Gandhi was also Pandit Nehru's daughter.

GYARAH MURTI

Moving down towards Willingdon Crescent from Moti Bagh, at the T-junction one can witness perhaps one of the finest sculptures ever to be made in the history of sculpting. For there stands the emblem of India's freedom struggle, the mark of Indian secularism, all being led by the Father of the Nation, Mahatma Gandhi. It was constructed by Devi Prasad Roy Choudhury as a tribute to Mahatma Gandhi, and the Dandi March that he had led way back in 1930 to protest against the salt monopoly carried out by the state. It is also a feature of Indian secularism, as members from all religions are seen marching there, following Mahatma Gandhi to their destination.

JANTAR MANTAR

In a quest for discovering the mysteries of the cosmos, Sawai Jai Singh-II built Jantar Mantar near the gates of City Palace, Jaipur, in India and then repeated the same feat at Delhi, right behind Barakhamba Road. It is a re-phrasal of the Sanskrit word 'yantra mantra' meaning instruments and formulae. The observatory has placement of huge masonry instruments - taking into account the position of the equator, sun, latitudes and longitudes, in order to verify the accuracy of the astronomical observations made. The sheer magnitude of the structure, coupled with the technological advancement made in that day and age alone make it a structural marvel. The Jantar Mantar manages to draw huge crowds even to this day.